Good Question!

Why Couldn't Susan B. Anthony Vote?

AND OTHER QUESTIONS ABOUT . . .

Women's Suffrage

STERLING CHILDREN'S BOOKS

New York

STERLING CHILDREN'S BOOKS
New York

An Imprint of Sterling Publishing
387 Park Avenue South
New York, NY 10016

Text © 2015 by Mary Kay Carson
Illustrations © 2015 Sterling Publishing Co., Inc.

ISBN 978-1-4549-1241-5 [hardcover]
ISBN 978-1-4549-1242-2 [paperback]

Distributed in Canada by Sterling Publishing
c/o Canadian Manda Group, 165 Dufferin Street
Toronto, Ontario, Canada M6K 3H6
Distributed in the United Kingdom by GMC Distribution Services
Castle Place, 166 High Street, Lewes, East Sussex, England BN7 1XU
Distributed in Australia by Capricorn Link (Australia) Pty. Ltd.
P.O. Box 704, Windsor, NSW 2756, Australia

Design by Andrea Miller
Art by Robert Hunt

For information about custom editions, special sales, and premium and corporate purchases,
please contact Sterling Special Sales at 800-805-5489 or specialsales@sterlingpublishing.com.

Manufactured in China
Lot #:
2 4 6 8 10 9 7 5 3 1
10/14

www.sterlingpublishing.com/kids

CONTENTS

Why couldn't Susan B. Anthony vote?

Susan B. Anthony helped make the United States a better country. She wanted all people to be treated fairly. Today we'd call her a social activist. In the 1800s, when Anthony lived, she was called a reformer. A reformer is someone devoted to bringing about change, or reform, to improve society.

The nineteenth century was a time of many reform movements in America. Susan B. Anthony worked alongside others to end slavery, fought to reform child labor, and sought restrictions on alcohol because of the problems it caused some families. But Susan B. Anthony was a woman. At that time, she could not be a governor or run for congress. As a woman, Anthony could not even vote. Not being able to vote meant that reformers like Anthony had little power to change things. The female half of America had no say in how their country was run. Their choices for presidents, senators, and town sheriffs didn't count. Anthony felt this was unfair and wrong. Changing that fact became her life's work.

Susan B. Anthony traveled across the country giving speeches and gathering signatures on formal requests sent to officials, called petitions. People made fun of Anthony and her new ideas. Leaders, clergy, and newspaper writers criticized her. She was arrested for attempting to vote. But Susan B. Anthony was a crusader. She battled for women's rights for more than half a century. Her dedication led to a huge change in America. Women became voters.

During the 1910s suffragists marched in parades to rally support for their right to vote.

Why is voting important?

Voting is how citizens shape their government. The United States has a government that rules by laws. Elected representatives make most of those laws. America is also a democracy, so the people get to choose their representatives. Senators, governors, mayors, and presidents are all voted into office by people in public elections. These elections decide who leads and who gets to make laws. Everyone is affected by the decisions elected officials make and the laws they create. That's why voting matters.

What is women's suffrage?

The nation's founders believed that Americans should govern themselves. They wrote a constitution that called for a president and a legislature, or a group who makes laws, who would be elected by the people. But they had a narrow view of who those voters should be. Suffrage is having the right to vote in public elections. Early suffrage was limited to white men aged twenty-one or older who owned land. That left out a lot of people—women, enslaved people, nonwhite immigrants, Native Americans, people of certain religions, and poor people who didn't own land. Who can and can't vote has changed throughout American history.

By the mid-1800s nearly all white men could vote in America. But those of other races and the entire female half of the population could not. Voting was only available to a minority of Americans until the twentieth century.

Women's suffrage is the right of women to vote. The women's suffrage movement sought equal voting rights for women. This was the goal of the so-called suffragists. Their struggle started in the early 1800s. It was a time when Americans began educating their daughters, not just their sons. Women were learning about social issues and joining in political discussions. But many women felt that their opinions carried no weight. Suffragists decided that the power to vote would help them gain other rights. Voting would allow them to better fight for issues that were important to them.

Susan Brownell Anthony was born in Massachusetts in 1820. When she was six, her family moved fifty miles to Battenville, New York, where her father ran cotton mills. Susan grew up with two brothers and four sisters. The Anthony family was part of the Quaker religious group, whose beliefs were different from most at the time. Quakers are pacifists, meaning they do not believe in war or violence for any reason. They also believe that men and women of all races are equal.

Quaker families wore plain clothes, didn't sing, dance, or drink alcohol. It's likely Susan's father didn't allow toys, games, or music in their house either. He believed these amusements kept the children from concentrating on God. Hard work was expected. From early girlhood Susan sewed, cooked, cleaned, and did other chores. She also worked in her father's mills sometimes. The Anthonys taught their children that being useful to the world was a Quaker's duty. "Go and do all the good you can," Susan's mother would say. Although the Anthony family was strict, they were caring and supportive. Susan's brothers later fought to end slavery, and her sisters became suffragists, too.

Who were the Quakers?

People who belong to the Religious Society of Friends are often called Quakers. The name of this Christian faith comes from their reputation of quaking or trembling with spirit during worship. Quakerism started in England, but many Quakers emigrated to America during the late 1600s. New England, Pennsylvania, Ohio, and Indiana all had large Quaker communities during the 1700–1800s. Quakers worked in many reform movements, including the abolition of slavery, better treatment of prisoners, and education for children of all races and sexes. They started many schools and universities. Today's Quakers are still involved in humanitarian work around the world.

FRIENDS MEETING HOUSE MERION.

Hugh Reinagle Pinx.ᵗ

Engraved by J.W. Steel.

Pub. by C.G.Childs Engraver 80 Walnut S.ᵗ Philadelphia ___ 1830.

Why did Susan's father take her out of school?

For most children in the early 1800s, school took place in a one-room schoolhouse. Kids as young as five learned alongside teenagers. While everyone shared the same classroom, students weren't all taught together. Boys sat on one side and girls sat on the other. Younger kids sat up front near the teacher, and older students sat in the back. The teacher, or schoolmaster, decided what each student learned. Everyone worked at their own level, and older kids often helped younger ones. Many schoolmasters had only finished eighth grade, and perhaps had trained for a few weeks learning how to teach.

Susan was an eager student and had learned to read before she turned four. She started going to class at the local school where her brothers and sisters went. One day Susan came home upset. According to a family story, the schoolmaster had refused to teach her long division because she was a girl. Maybe the male teacher felt girls didn't need to learn such advanced math. Many people back then believed that too much learning harmed girls' brains and would make them bad mothers. Or perhaps the schoolmaster was covering up for not knowing how to do long division himself. Either way, Susan's father pulled her out of school. As a Quaker, he believed all children should receive equal education.

Mr. Anthony started a home school for his kids and the girls who worked in his mills. He hired Mary Perkins, a well-educated woman who used modern teaching methods. She taught the children to recite poems and showed them books with pictures—things they wouldn't do in regular school. Each student even had his or her own stool to sit on—no more squeezing together on long benches. Female teachers weren't common in the early 1800s. Perkins was likely the first educated and independent unmarried woman Susan had ever met. Susan's teacher was a new kind of role model for young women. Susan studied with Perkins until age seventeen, when her father sent her to a Quaker boarding school in Philadelphia.

Why was Susan fired from her first job?

Hard times hit the Anthony family during the late 1830s. The country fell into an economic depression, and Susan's family lost everything. The mills closed and their nice brick home had to be auctioned off. With no money to pay tuition, teenaged Susan had to end her studies at boarding school. Her family was renting an old tavern in Hardscrabble, New York. They made ends meet by putting up travelers and renting out rooms. To help her family earn more money, she left at age nineteen to find work as a teacher.

Her first job didn't last long. When Anthony realized that the male teachers were paid four or five times more than the female teachers, she complained. It got her fired. Susan found other jobs, though, and eventually became the headmistress of Canajoharie Academy's girls' department. Anthony earned a living as a respected teacher for ten years. But she began to feel unsatisfied. She wanted to do more with her life, make a bigger difference. So at age twenty-nine, Anthony quit her job. As a reformer, Anthony wanted to make the world better. She started by taking up the cause of temperance.

What was the temperance movement?

Reformers like Susan B. Anthony saw drinking alcohol as a moral issue. They believed that alcohol abuse destroyed families. It harmed people's health, bred poverty, and made workplaces unsafe. The temperance movement called for a ban on alcohol. Temperance was closely tied to the women's rights movement. Women were often victims of men's alcoholism. Drunken men would beat their wives and kids and drive families into poverty by spending money on alcohol and being unfit to work. But women could do little about it. Wife beating wasn't a crime, and women had limited rights to divorce their husbands or gain custody of their children. Susan B. Anthony worked in the temperance movement in New York. She attended rallies against alcohol, but was not allowed to speak because of her sex.

The ideas of the temperance movement showed up in popular books and plays, like *The Drunkard*. Newspapers printed cartoons and illustrations showing women fighting the evils of alcohol.

Who was Elizabeth Cady Stanton?

Elizabeth Cady Stanton came from a well-off family and was an educated woman. She married an abolitionist leader, and together they attended the 1840 World Anti-Slavery Convention in London, England. Stanton was shocked to find that women weren't allowed to speak at the convention. Female attendees even had to sit apart from the men. How could abolitionists seeking rights for enslaved people not want the same rights for their daughters, mothers, sisters, and wives? Stanton knew then that only by voting could women obtain their rights.

Susan B. Anthony and Elizabeth Cady Stanton first met in 1851. The two became fast friends and worked together for the next fifty years. Stanton was a keen thinker and skilled writer. She was also the mother of seven children. Anthony had the energy and freedom to travel and give talks, but struggled with putting her ideas into words. Stanton wrote most of the suffrage speeches and petitions that Anthony would deliver. "I forged the thunderbolts, she fired them," said Stanton. It was a partnership that forever changed the world.

What happened at Seneca Falls, New York, in 1848?

A few years before she met Anthony, Stanton and fellow abolitionist Lucretia Mott got to talking during the 1840 World Anti-Slavery Convention. Neither liked being silenced because of their sex, so they decided to hold a convention of their own. The result was the first Woman's Rights Convention in the United States. Mott and Stanton held it in Seneca Falls, New York, on July 19–20, 1848. About three hundred people attended, most of them women. They listened as Stanton read the "Declaration of Sentiments." The document she had written updated phrases from the Declaration of Independence. "All men are created equal" was changed to "all men and women are created equal." Stanton's speech called for women to be able to own property, sign contracts, attend college, and keep the money they earned. But the most radical idea that Stanton proposed during the convention was voting rights for women. The suffrage movement was heating up.

In 1848 Elizabeth Cady Stanton spoke at the first Woman's Rights Convention in Seneca Falls, New York.

THE BLOOMER COSTUME.

Wearing bloomers instead of long dresses made
walking, chores, and other activities easier for women.

What were bloomers?

Proper dress was part of being a respectable woman in the nineteenth century. Even while gardening or hanging up laundry, women wore heavy dresses with layers of petticoats over painfully tight corsets. Skirts reached all the way to the floor, so they would drag through dirt and mud; women had to hold up their skirts while walking anywhere.

Wearing more practical, less restrictive clothing became a symbol of the women's movement for a time. A cousin of Elizabeth Cady Stanton's invented an outfit made up of a shorter dress with loose pants underneath. The pants came to be known as "bloomers" because suffragist Amelia Bloomer promoted the outfit in her newspaper. Stanton and Anthony wore bloomers and also cut their hair short. Bloomer-wearing women were horribly ridiculed in newspapers and laughed at and criticized on the street. Stanton's father wouldn't allow Elizabeth to visit if she was wearing bloomers. Anthony and others gave it up after a year or so. They felt it got them attention for the wrong reasons and gave people an excuse to not take women's rights seriously.

Did Susan B. Anthony ever marry?

The women's rights movement was about more than voting. Married women had few rights. The husband owned everything in a marriage. Wives couldn't own land, the house they lived in, or any wages that they earned. They didn't own the clothing on their backs, or even the garden vegetables they grew. Wives belonged to their husbands, and children belonged to their fathers. Only in rare instances could a wife divorce a husband and also keep her children. Only men could request a divorce. While she was teaching, Susan B. Anthony dated and had men propose to her. But Anthony knew that marriage meant giving up her independence. The causes she fought for, and her own interests, would come second to a husband. "I never felt I could give up my life of freedom to become a man's housekeeper," she wrote.

Why was the Fifteenth Amendment so disappointing to the suffragists?

The fight to end slavery had been part of Susan B. Anthony's life from early on. Like many Quaker families, the Anthonys were abolitionists. They held anti-slavery meetings at their home. Susan B. Anthony began working for the American Anti-Slavery Society in 1856. She arranged meetings, made speeches, put up posters, handed out leaflets, and was threatened by pro-slavery mobs.

As reformers, most people in the women's rights movement were also involved in anti-slavery efforts. It was no coincidence. Rights for the enslaved and rights for women were connected in many minds. If one person should not own another person, then that also extended to wives being the property of their husbands. If people of all races should be educated citizens, why couldn't women go to college?

When the Civil War ended and slavery was abolished in 1865, African Americans were far from equal members of society. Black people couldn't even vote. When reformers pushed for voting rights for African Americans, Anthony and others called for something more. They wanted universal suffrage—the right of all races and sexes to vote.

A few years after the Civil War ended, the government changed the U.S. Constitution. They added an amendment, or change, to the nation's most important set of laws. The Fifteenth Amendment granted voting rights to African Americans—but just men. Suffragists were furious and felt betrayed. They'd fought to end slavery, but didn't get any support for women's rights in turn. "Many abolitionists have yet to learn the ABC of woman's rights," wrote Anthony. She and Stanton realized change would have to be up to women themselves. In 1869 Anthony and Stanton formed the National Woman Suffrage Association. Men could join, but couldn't be leaders in the group. Susan B. Anthony began working for a different change to the Constitution—an amendment that guaranteed all women the right to vote.

The caption of this 1911 newspaper cartoon read: SIGNING THE DECLARATION OF THEIR INDEPENDENCE. It made fun of the suffrage movement and suffragists, including Susan B. Anthony, who is shown in a black dress seated at the table.

The cartoon copies a famous painting (at right) of the Founding Fathers and the Declaration of Independence. The artist has drawn the women in bloomers and other men's clothing to make them look ridiculous and overly serious.

How did Susan B. Anthony fight for women's suffrage?

The fact that women couldn't vote made fighting for their rights extra difficult. Women couldn't vote pro-suffrage leaders into office. Politicians serve the people who elect them, and those people didn't include women. Suffragists needed the backing of the American public. Opening minds and changing opinions were the tools that Susan B. Anthony used to gain their support. She was a tireless speaker. Anthony spent decades traveling from one town to another giving lectures. Her most famous lecture, "Woman Wants Bread, Not the Ballot," challenged her opponents head-on. Many believed that women only cared about feeding their families and had no interest in elections. Anthony argued that her lecture's title—and the idea—was wrong. She said that voting, or giving them the ballot, was a woman's only way of "securing bread and a home for herself."

Anthony was often scorned, and her talks were criticized. One newspaperman called her lectures "devilish" and out to "poison the morals of . . . wives, mothers and daughters." Strangers called her hateful names and made fun of how she looked and spoke. One of her talks was sabotaged by boys dumping spicy hot pepper powder onto a hot stove, right outside the room where she was speaking. When the spice started burning, everyone left coughing from the fumes.

While suffragists didn't have radio, television, or the Internet to help them spread the word, magazines did exist. Susan B. Anthony published a weekly journal called *The Revolution* from 1868 to 1870. It demanded equal rights for women. The motto printed on its front page read: "The true republic—men, their rights and nothing more; women, their rights and nothing less."

Susan B. Anthony also worked to change laws. In 1877 she presented the U.S. Congress with suffrage petitions from twenty-six states with ten thousand signatures. She became one of the first female American politicians. Anthony traveled to Washington, D.C., every year through the late 1800s to ask Congress to pass a suffrage amendment. They told her "no" more than thirty times.

Why was Susan B. Anthony arrested in 1872?

The Fifteenth Amendment gave citizens the right to vote no matter their "race, color, or previous condition of servitude." Suffragists argued that since they were citizens and came in all races and colors, the amendment included women. All they needed was to get the Supreme Court to agree. When a criminal court decides someone is guilty, the guilty party can appeal, asking for a higher court to change the decision. As the highest court, the Supreme Court has the final say. Suffragists urged women across the nation to try to vote during the 1872 presidential election. The plan was to appeal the guilty verdicts of women arrested to the Supreme Court.

Susan B. Anthony and her sisters were among a group of fifty women demanding to register to vote in Rochester, New York. After voting for president Ulysses S. Grant, Anthony wrote her friend Elizabeth Cady Stanton to say, "I have been and gone and done it!" Two weeks later a deputy U.S. Marshal arrested Anthony. Her crime? Knowingly voting while female.

Susan B. Anthony did not get a fair trial. The judge wouldn't let Anthony speak in court, or testify. He said women were incompetent, and not smart or trustworthy enough. The judge also didn't allow the all-male jury to discuss the case. He told them to find her guilty. He fined Anthony one hundred dollars, but refused to jail her when she wouldn't pay it—this prevented the case from going on to the Supreme Court, which he knew was the suffragists' ultimate goal. Many considered the trial "a mere farce." The trial made headlines, and Anthony ensured that newspapers across the country got copies of what was said in the court. It convinced many Americans that women were being treated unfairly. Two years later, another woman who had tried to vote did get her case heard by the Supreme Court. But the court decided against her, saying that women didn't get to vote just because they were citizens. The Supreme Court also said that it was up to each state to decide who could and couldn't vote.

While not allowed to speak during the trial, Anthony was asked during sentencing if she had anything to say. Anthony stunned the courtroom by arguing that her rights had been trampled. She said that the laws were "all made by men, interpreted by men, administered by men, in favor of men, and against women."

Women in the
Wyoming Territory
could vote as early
as 1869. When
Wyoming became
a state in 1890, it
was the first to give
women the vote.

Did any state allow women to vote?

The Supreme Court's ruling that each state had to decide who could vote weakened the Fifteenth Amendment. Southern states started making up all kinds of rules to keep once-enslaved men from voting. Black voters had to own property, pass a reading test, or pay a special fee. Susan B. Anthony had seen it coming. This is what happens when you deny universal suffrage, she said. Not only were women denied the vote, but so were many of the African American men the Fifteenth Amendment was written for.

But women's rights workers also took advantage of the new power of states. Some western territories had been allowing women to vote, including Wyoming, Colorado, Utah, and Idaho. Anthony traveled far from home during the late 1800s to help western women earn at least some voting rights. Not all of these states gave full voting rights to women. Some allowed voting only in local or state elections. Still, it was something. It proved that women were responsible voters.

By the turn of the century, Susan B. Anthony had become an honored public figure. Theodore Roosevelt himself congratulated her on her eighty-sixth birthday in 1906. But true as always to the cause, she objected to the compliment. "I would rather have President Roosevelt say one word to Congress in favor of amending the Constitution to give women the suffrage than to praise me endlessly!" Anthony knew she wouldn't be there to see victory herself. Her health was failing. Elizabeth Cady Stanton had already died in 1902. A new generation was leading the battle now. Anthony had no doubt that they would see it through. These women are "true and devoted to the cause," she told those gathered in honor of her eighty-sixth birthday. "Failure is impossible." A few weeks later, Susan B. Anthony died at home in Rochester, New York, on March 13, 1906.

Why were suffragist protesters force-fed in jail?

When America entered World War I in 1917, women stepped up to help. Thousands served as nurses and worked in factories making weapons. As World War I raged in Europe, the battle for women's voting rights heated up, too. Suffragists were growing impatient, tired of such slow progress. Their soldiers were dying for Europe's freedom, yet at home they didn't have the freedom of voting.

Susan B. Anthony had first asked for a suffrage amendment to the Constitution nearly a half century earlier. The time for talking was over. Young suffragist leaders like Alice Paul and Lucy Burns wanted action, so they organized marches called suffrage parades. Tens of thousands of women of all colors and classes, dressed in white, flooded the streets in Washington, D.C., and New York. In early 1917, protestors stationed themselves permanently in front of the White House. They held picket signs or banners that displayed suffrage messages like "Mr. President, How Long Must Women Wait for Liberty?"

That summer, police began arresting the picketers for blocking the sidewalk. Nearly five hundred women were arrested and 168 were jailed. When Alice Paul was arrested, authorities threatened to lock her up in a mental hospital—hoping to convince the public she was insane. Many suffragists were treated horribly in jail—punched and pushed around, and thrown into cold, dirty, rat-infested cells. In protest, the women refused to eat. Their hunger strikes were met with force-feedings. Three times a day, jailers shoved a hose down each prisoner's throat and poured liquids into her stomach. But the abuse backfired. Once word of this treatment got out, the public was shocked and outraged. Congress called for investigations into the abuse. Courts declared the arrests illegal, and all the suffragists were freed. News of what happened to the jailed women covered front pages of newspapers. The suffragists would no longer be ignored and put off. In 1918 President Woodrow Wilson declared his support of a suffrage amendment.

VOTES FOR WOMEN A SUCCESS

The Map Proves It

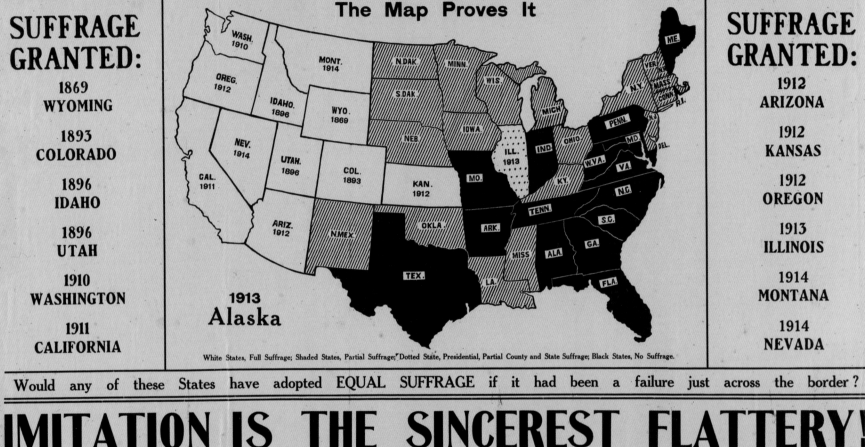

SUFFRAGE GRANTED:

1869
WYOMING

1893
COLORADO

1896
IDAHO

1896
UTAH

1910
WASHINGTON

1911
CALIFORNIA

SUFFRAGE GRANTED:

1912
ARIZONA

1912
KANSAS

1912
OREGON

1913
ILLINOIS

1914
MONTANA

1914
NEVADA

1913
Alaska

White States, Full Suffrage; Shaded States, Partial Suffrage; Dotted State, Presidential, Partial County and State Suffrage; Black States, No Suffrage.

Would any of these States have adopted EQUAL SUFFRAGE if it had been a failure just across the border?

IMITATION IS THE SINCEREST FLATTERY!

National Woman Suffrage Publishing Company, Inc., 505 Fifth Avenue, New York

This 1914 map shows the states with full voting rights for women in white and no suffrage for women in black. The lined and dotted states only allowed women to vote in some elections, usually just local ones.

What is the Nineteenth Amendment?

In 1918, the House of Representatives met to decide on women's suffrage. All kinds of people turned out to watch the vote. Could the suffragists get the 274 votes needed to create an amendment to the Constitution? Representative Frederick C. Hicks of New York left his dying wife to go to Washington for the vote. She had asked him to. Without his vote, it is likely that the amendment's creation wouldn't have been approved by the House of Representatives. Unfortunately, it took the Senate more than a year to join the House in approving the amendment. Four decades after Susan B. Anthony first wrote and introduced the amendment giving women the vote, it passed in both the Senate and House on June 4, 1919. All it needed was approval by three-fourths of the states. In 1919 there were forty-eight states, so the suffragists needed thirty-six states to approve, or ratify, the amendment. Then they would finally have the vote. Within ten months, thirty-five states had ratified it. It would take another five months to get the crucial thirty-sixth state.

The Tennessee summer of 1920 was long and hot. Suffragists poured into the capital city of Nashville for the vote on August 18. They and their supporters wore yellow roses to identify themselves. Nashville also swarmed with people opposed to women voting. They wore red roses. It all came down to the youngest member of the Tennessee assembly, Harry T. Burn. The twenty-four-year-old stood up to vote wearing a red rose in his lapel. Burn had planned on voting no. But in his pocket was a letter from his mother asking him to vote yes. He followed her advice. The Nineteenth Amendment was now a law, stating: "The right of citizens of the United States to vote shall not be denied or abridged by the United States or by any state on account of sex."

Do all women around the world have the right to vote?

One hundred years after Susan B. Anthony's birth, all American women were finally able to vote. On November 2, 1920, women in all forty-eight states voted for president. Newspaper headlines announced, "Women by Thousands Pour Into Polling Places." The female voters helped elect Warren G. Harding the twenty-ninth president of the United States.

Susan B. Anthony didn't live to see women get the vote in America. But other nations did grant full female suffrage in her lifetime. New Zealand granted voting rights equal to men in 1893. Women in many European countries could vote before the Nineteenth Amendment gave women in the United States their full voting rights.

Although American women weren't first, they were far from last. Women in Kazakhstan couldn't vote until 1994, and Kuwait didn't have female suffrage until 2005. Some countries continue to deny women voting rights. Suffrage is limited for both men and women in the United Arab Emirates. In Lebanon, women—but not men—must prove they have completed elementary school to vote. The struggle for equal rights between men and women goes on around the globe. If Susan B. Anthony were alive today, she would no doubt be working to change that. There is still good to do and ways to be useful to the world.

In 1979 and 1980 the U.S. government minted $1 coins with Susan B. Anthony's picture. She was the first woman to be shown on a United States coin.

A monument to Susan B. Anthony, Elizabeth Cady Stanton, and Lucretia Mott stands today in the rotunda of the United States Capitol in Washington, D.C.